active minds
EXPLORERS

My Sense of
HEARING

Tweet tweet

I'm listening.

Ellen Lawrence

sequoia
kids media

Sound waves ♪ 𝄞

When you strum a guitar, the sound waves travel away from the guitar in every direction.

Consultant:
Suzy Gazlay, MA
Recipient, Presidential Award for Excellence in Science Teaching

Photography © Shutterstock 2023 Aleks Melnik; Alexandra Dikaia; Anastasia Tveretinova; Anatoliy Karlyuk; Ania Samoilova; Astarina; balabolka; Barks; bsd studio; Daniela Barreto; dimpank; Ermak Oksana; Fafarumba; Goodreason; HardtIllustrations; hchjjl; jackhollingsworth.com; Kin_Taburo; Lemon Workshop Design; lena_nikolaeva; LHF Graphics; LintangDesign; mady70; magicoven; Magomed Magomedagaev; Master1305; mhatzapa; miha de; mijatmijatovic; monoo; Net Vector; Netkoff; Nik Merkulov; noir_illustration; Nopparat Promtha; Palau; Pics Garden; Pixel-Shot; prochasson frederic; Receh Lancar Jaya; Roman Malyshev; Samuel Borges Photography; suerz; Tartila; VALUA VITALY; Vasin Lee; vitdes; Zaiets Svitlana
Additional photography provided by Ruby Tuesday Books: SuperStock (p. 11); Stocktrek Images/SuperStock (p. 13); The National Deaf Children's Society (p. 16)

Published by Sequoia Kids Media,
an imprint of Sequoia Publishing & Media, LLC

Sequoia Publishing & Media, LLC,
a division of Phoenix International Publications, Inc.

8501 West Higgins Road
Chicago, Illinois 60631

© 2024 Sequoia Publishing & Media, LLC
First published © Ruby Tuesday Books Limited

CustomerService@PhoenixInternational.com

Sequoia Kids Media and associated logo are trademarks and/or registered trademarks of Sequoia Publishing & Media, LLC.

Active Minds is a registered trademark of Phoenix International Publications, Inc. and is used with permission.

www.SequoiaKidsMedia.com

Library of Congress Control Number: 2023935324

ISBN: 979-8-7654-0297-9

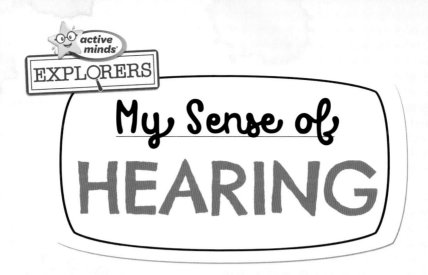

Table of Contents

Words shown in **bold** in the text are
explained in the glossary.

Sounds All Around

When you listen to music, your **sense** of hearing is helping you have fun.

RING! RING! RING!

When you hear the alarm go off during a school fire drill, your hearing is keeping you safe.

Every day, you hear thousands of different sounds.

Cock-a-doodle-doo!

GO! GO! GO!

It's not just your ears doing the hearing, though.

A whole team of body parts is working together to collect and **process** these sounds.

BOOM!

What exactly are sounds, though, and how are you able to hear them?

Tweet!

Your body has five senses. These are seeing, hearing, smelling, tasting, and touching. Your senses help keep you safe. They also help you enjoy the world around you.

VROOM!

How Are Sounds Made?

TWANG!

If you strum the strings of a guitar, you will hear twangy sounds.

How are those sounds being made?

Strumming the guitar strings makes them vibrate, or move very fast.

As they move, they create **vibrations** in the air.

These vibrations in the air are called **sound waves**.

BOOM!

5 seconds

1 mile (1.6 km)

Sound waves travel very fast. In fact, they can travel one mile (1.6 kilometers) in just five seconds!

Your ears collect these waves and, in less than a second, turn them into sounds!

When you strum a guitar, the sound waves travel away from the guitar in every direction.

WOOF! WOOF! WOOF! WOOF! WOOF!

Sound waves

This picture shows how sound waves act. You can't actually see sound waves in the air, though.

I hear you!

Ears in Action

Every noise you hear is made up of sound waves traveling through the air.

The part of your ear that sticks out from your head collects these sound waves.

Then it guides them into a tube called an **ear canal**.

Having an ear on each side of your head allows you to hear better than if you only had one ear.

That's because your two ears can collect sound waves coming at you from both sides.

The part of your ear that you can see is called the **pinna**. It is made from a tough, rubbery **tissue** called **cartilage**.

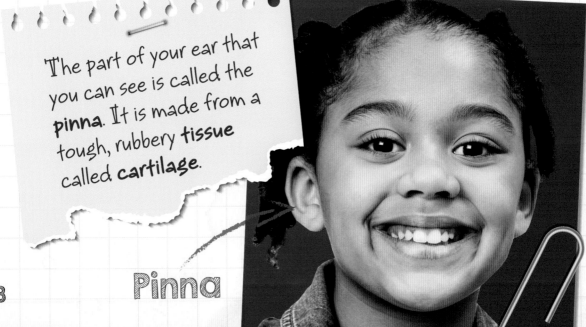

Pinna

This picture shows the parts of your ear that are deep inside your head.

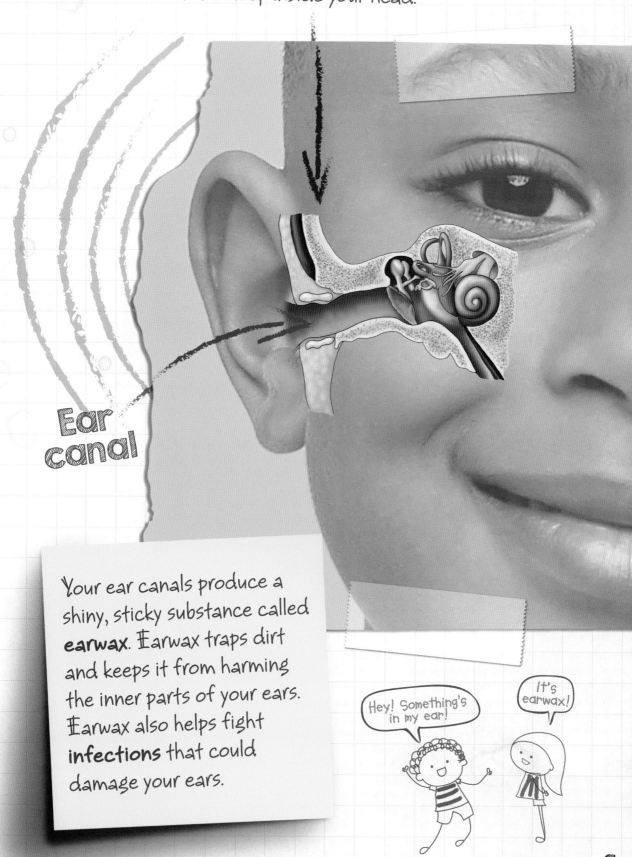

Ear canal

Your ear canals produce a shiny, sticky substance called **earwax**. Earwax traps dirt and keeps it from harming the inner parts of your ears. Earwax also helps fight **infections** that could damage your ears.

Hey! Something's in my ear!

It's earwax!

Vibrations on the Move

Sound waves travel down your ear canal until they hit your **eardrum**.

Your eardrum is a piece of skin that is stretched tight across the ear canal.

The sound waves make your eardrum vibrate.

Good vibrations!

Your eardrum is a little like the tightly stretched top of a drum.

Then your eardrum passes on the vibrations to a tiny bone called the malleus.

The malleus moves and hits another bone called the incus.

Finally, the incus passes on the vibrations to the tiny stapes bone.

Malleus! Incus! Stapes!

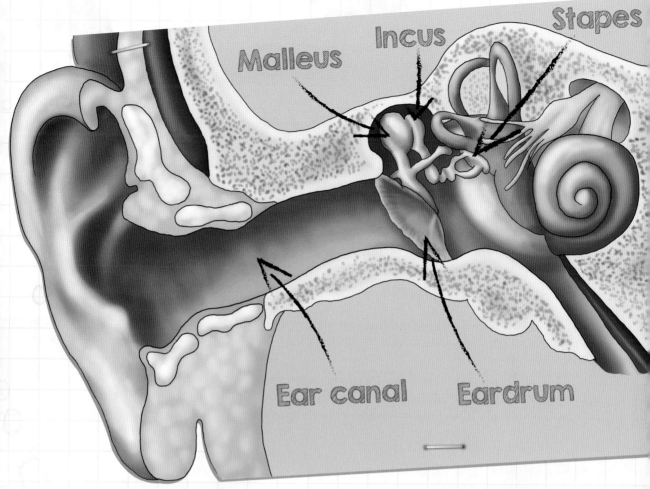

Malleus Incus Stapes

Ear canal Eardrum

The malleus, incus, and stapes are also called the hammer, anvil, and stirrup. They are the three smallest bones in your body.

This picture shows the size of your three ear bones compared to a dime.

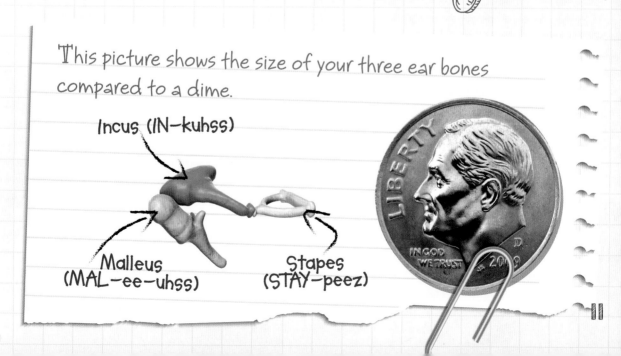

Incus (IN-kuhss)

Malleus (MAL-ee-uhss)

Stapes (STAY-peez)

Here Come the Sounds

I hear ya!

Your eardrum passes vibrations from the malleus to the incus to the stapes.

Next, the tiny stapes bone vibrates against a part of your ear called the **cochlea**.

The cochlea is filled with liquid and contains **cells with tiny hairs** on them.

A cochlea looks like a tiny, curled snail shell.

STAPES

The vibrations from the stapes make ripples in the liquid inside the cochlea.

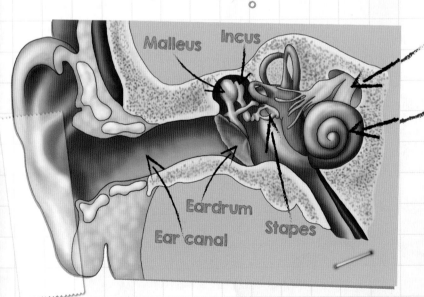

Malleus

Incus

Eardrum

Ear canal

Stapes

Nerve cells

Cochlea

The tiny hairs are moved by the ripples and turn the movements into messages.

Then the hairs send the messages through **nerve cells** to your brain.

Your cochlea contains about 15,000 tiny hairs. They are so small, you can't see them with your eyes.

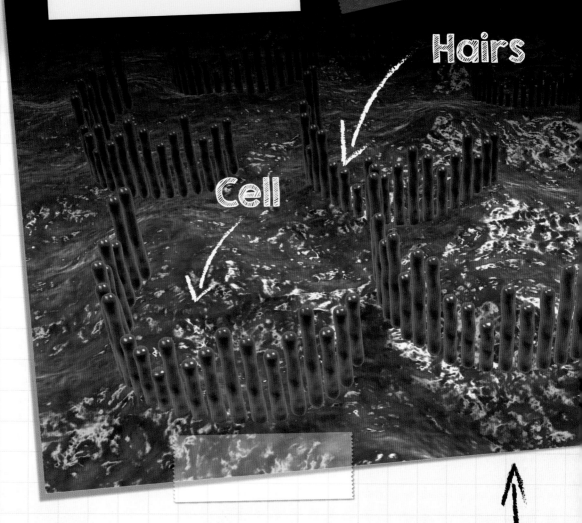

Hairs

Cell

WOW!

This photo was created by a **microscope**. It shows the hairs inside a person's cochlea. In the photo, the hairs are thousands of times bigger than in real life.

Your Brain Gets to Work

The messages from your cochlea travel along nerve cells to your brain.

In an instant, your brain gets to work.

It processes the messages, and you hear a sound.

WOOF!
WOOF!

From a dog's bark to music, every noise you hear is just a vibration in the air.

Your amazing sense of hearing, however, turns these vibrations into sounds.

Your Amazing Sense of Hearing

1 A person plays a guitar.

2 Sound waves move through the air and are collected by your ears.

3 Inside your ears, the waves are turned into messages that are sent to your brain.

4 Your brain turns the messages into the sound of music.

Help with Hearing

Not everyone hears in the same way.

Some people have **hearing loss** because an injury or illness affects their ears.

Some people are born with hearing loss.

A person with hearing loss might be able to hear some sounds, but not others.

Some people cannot hear any sounds at all.

There are ways that some people with hearing loss can improve their hearing.

Hearing aid

Some people's ears need help in passing vibrations to the cochlea. Wearing a hearing aid can help people's ears do this. Then they hear sounds more easily. Most hearing aids are worn on the outside part of the ear.

Some people with damaged cochleas have an operation. A doctor puts a tiny piece of electronic equipment called a cochlear implant into a person's cochlea. The implant then does the work of the cochlea, helping the person hear.

I can hear you now!

These pieces of equipment help the cochlear implant work.

Amazing Ears

Your ears don't just help you hear, they also help you stay balanced.

Deep inside each of your ears are three small loops filled with liquid and tiny hairs.

If you tilt your head to one side, the liquid in the loops moves, too.

The tiny hairs are moved by the liquid and turn the movements into messages.

The messages tell your brain that your head is now tilted to one side.

Then your brain can tell the rest of your body to stay balanced, so you don't fall sideways!

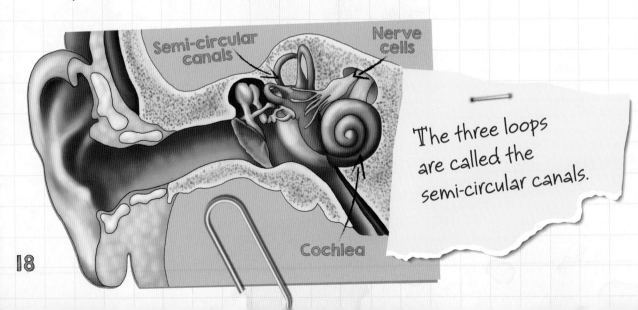

Semi-circular canals

Nerve cells

Cochlea

The three loops are called the semi-circular canals.

I'm dizzy!

If you spin around and then stop, you will feel dizzy. This happens because the liquid in your ears keeps moving.

Because the liquid is moving, your ears keep on sending messages to your brain that you're spinning. Your brain knows that your body isn't spinning, though.

For a few seconds, your brain is confused. It's this confusion in your brain that makes you feel dizzy!

Take Care of Your Ears

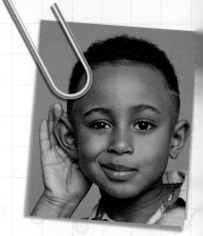

Watch out!

Without your sense of hearing, you couldn't hear music, movies, or people talking.

Your hearing keeps you safe by allowing you to hear cars, fire alarms, or someone shouting a warning.

It's good to know, therefore, that there's a lot you can do to keep your ears healthy.

Don't stick anything in me!

The most important thing to remember is never to poke anything into your ear!

This could harm your ear canal or eardrum.

Taking good care of your ears will help you keep on enjoying your amazing sense of hearing.

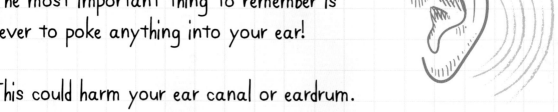

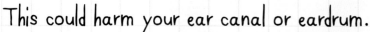

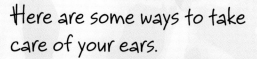

Here are some ways to take care of your ears.

Earwax will wash out of your ears on its own when you wash your hair. NEVER poke a cotton swab, finger, or other object into your ear to remove earwax.

Very loud sounds can damage your ears. When you wear earphones, keep the volume turned down low.

If your ears hurt, or you are having trouble hearing, tell a grown-up. Then you can arrange to visit a doctor and get an ear check-up.

Glossary

cartilage (KAR-tuh-lij)
Strong, rubbery tissue found in many areas of the body, including your nose and ears.

cells (SELZ)
Very tiny parts of a living thing. Your bones, muscles, skin, hair, and every part of you are made of cells.

cochlea (KOKE-lee-uh)
The part of your inner ear that contains liquid and hairs that send messages to your brain and help create sounds. It is shaped like a snail shell.

ear canal (EER kuh-NAL)
A narrow tube that connects the outside part of your ear to the inner parts of your ear.

eardrum (EER-druhm)
A piece of skin that is stretched tight across your ear canal, like the tightly stretched top of a drum. When sound waves hit your eardrum, it vibrates and makes it possible for you to hear sounds.

earwax (EER-waks)
A sticky, shiny substance that is produced by your ear canals. Earwax helps protect the insides of your ears from dirt and infections.

hearing loss (HEER-eeng LAWSS)
Being unable to hear some sounds or all sounds. Hearing loss happens if one or more parts of a person's ears are not working as they should.

infections (in-FEK-shuhnz)
Illnesses that are caused by germs entering the body.

microscope (MIKE-ruh-skope)
A tool or machine that is used to see things that are too small for people to see with their eyes alone.

nerve cells (NURV SELZ)
The billions of tiny cells that carry information back and forth between your brain and other parts of your body.

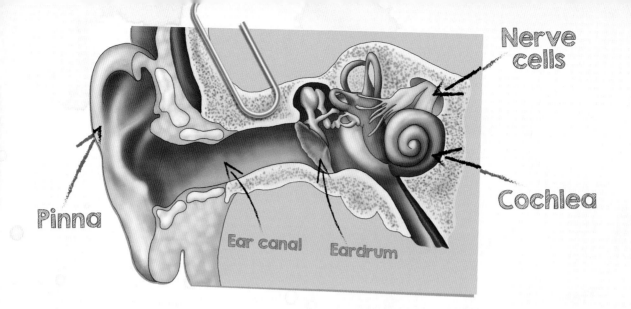

Nerve cells

Cochlea

Pinna

Ear canal

Eardrum

pinna (PIH-nuh)
The part of your ear that sticks out from the side of your head. It is made from cartilage.

process (PRAH-sess)
To carry out a step-by-step series of actions in order to make something happen.

sense (SENSS)
One of the five ways that you collect information about the world around you. Your senses are seeing, hearing, smelling, tasting, and touching.

sound waves (SOUND WAYVZ)
Vibrations that are collected by your ears and turned into sounds.

tissue (TISH-yoo)
A group of connected cells in your body that work together. Cells are very tiny parts of a living thing. Skin tissue, for example, is made up of skin cells.

vibrations (vy-BRAY-shuhnz)
Small, shaking movements that make something move back and forth, or side to side, quickly.

23

Index

Read More

My Little Book about Me
Angela Royston
London: Quarto Library (2022).

A Journey Through the Human Body
Steve Parker
Beverly, MA: Quarto Library (2022).

Visit Us

www.SequoiaKidsMedia.com
Downloadable content and more!